Taking Back God's Rainbow

TRUE REVELATION

Written by Veronica Gonzales
Illustrated by Jason Velazquez

His Glory Kingdom

San Antonio, Texas

My Dad, for receiving the Holy Spirit. Leading us to Jesus and never giving up on me by praying. I love you Dad and I know I had questions on how you left this earth, but the Lord is faithful, and he makes beauty from ashes.

My Mommy, words can't explain how you loved us all. Always encouraging me to never give up and always reminding me to be kind. Now I understand mommy how to be an older sister and an aunt to my family. I love you mommy I know you are in a wonderful place in paradise with Jesus with no more pain mommy.

My Godmother Guerrero Family, for blessing me as a child and speaking over my life by saying "May the love of God never depart from me," I love you always!

Lopez Family, being my spiritual father and mother. Always praying for me even when I was out of the will of the father, always showing me love, and never judging me. I Love you both always!

My Sister, Hudlin Family having a praying sister in my life always praying for me to return to the love of the father. To have a sister like you smart and as a godly woman breaking forth the way for our family. Words can't explain how thankful I am for you sis for never giving up on me. Love you little sister!

My sister's and brother Gonzales Family, always encouraging me in this season and in times of doubt. Love you all my family, God is faithful!

My friend Ms. Avalos, words can't explain how I appreciate everything you have done for me. In my darkest moments being there and still here now being free in the light with Jesus. Letting Jesus transform our lives with his mercy and grace. We our free sister in Christ Jesus with God, all things are possible. I love you my sister, blessing always!

Meier Family and Van Klaveren Family, you have so much love for God and by hearing his voice I know this was the right time and season for this to come to pass. I thank you Jesus for this Kairos moment and bringing these women warriors full of faith across my life. This is just the beginning; God is with us! I love you both!

Most of all to my Jesus, my Savior for pulling me out and setting me free and with your appointed time for the first book to go fourth all for his glory. LET THE HEAVENS TOUCH THE EARTH IN JESUS NAME!!!

R stands for Righteousness. God loves His children and created the rainbow to show His promises for the world. Be kind and do right because the Father loves you, and you are precious to Him. God, who created us, Jesus, the Son of God, and the Holy Spirit. Jesus gives us the Holy Spirit of joy, love, kindness, and peace.

Philippians 1:11 says, "Filled with the fruit of righteousness that comes through Jesus Christ to the glory and praise of God" (NIV).

R

A stands for authority. You have the authority in life to say no to evil. Think about how Jesus loves you and died on the cross for you. Pray to Jesus, He hears your prayers. You are strong and have strength in Jesus. Evil means something bad, and it is not of Jesus.

Matthew 28:18 says, "Then Jesus came to them and said, 'All authority in heaven and on earth has been given to me'" (NIV).

A

I stands for Identity. God created you in His image as either a boy, a young male, or a girl, a young female. True love and freedom comes from the Father. Through the eyes of Jesus, He loves and cares for you very much, and you are His child.

Mark 10:6 says, "But at the beginning of creation God made them male and female" (NIV).

N stands for New creation, God knew you before you were even born, children, Jesus went to the cross for you, and He loves you, You are the creation of God,

2 Corinthians 5:17 says, "Therefore, if anyone is in Christ, the new creation has come. The old has gone, the new is here!" (NIV).

N

B stands for Beautiful Boldness. Jesus is saying, "I love you, my children. I created you, and you are beautiful." Believe Him when He says you're beautiful, strong, and courageous. Strong means you have strength in Christ Jesus. Courageous is to be brave, Jesus is with you.

2 Timothy 1:7 says, "For God hath not given us the spirit of fear; but of power, and of love, and of a sound mind" (KJV).

B

O stands for original, children, original means this is your birth right in Jesus. You are created in the image of God. The seven colors of the rainbow means freedom for His children.

Genesis 1:27 says, "So God created mankind in his own image, in the image of God he created them; male and female he created them" (NIV).

Wstands for Willing Heart. Jesus gave His life for us on the cross. He gives you His heart. The love He has for you is to be free. Children, you will have victory in the land. God loves you; He just wants your whole heart. Willing heart means joy. When you receive a gift Jesus has given you, it's a gift of happiness. The heartbeat of Jesus is that He loves you.

1 John 4:16 says, "And so we know and rely on the love God has for us. God is love. Whoever lives in love lives in God, and God in them" (NIV).